mel bay presents

christmas solos for beginning violin

level 1
by craig duncan

Contents

	Violin	Piano
Angels We Have Heard on High	5	5
Away in a Manger	10	12
Deck the Halls	13	17
Ding, Dong Merrily on High	7	7
The First Nowell	4	4
Good King Wenceslas	6	6
Here We Come A-Wassailing	15	19
The Holly and the Ivy	14	18
Jingle Bells	11	14
Joy to the World	3	3
O Come, All Ye Faithful	12	16
Once in Royal David's City	8	9
The Rocking Carol	8	8
Silent Night	9	10
We Wish You a Merry Christmas	16	20
While Shepherds Watched Their Flocks	9	11

These arrangements have been designed to be enjoyed in a number of settings. There are companion books for viola and cello. Each book has the melody and a harmony part, along with piano accompaniment. Suggested uses are:

1. Solo violin with piano accompaniment.
2. Violin duets.
3. Violin and cello duets and trios with the cello book.
4. String quartet using the melody and harmony parts in the violin book, and the harmony parts in the viola and cello books. The cello book can also be played by a bass.

Joy to the World

George Frederick Handel

The First Nowell

English Carol

4

Angels We Have Heard on High

French Carol

Good King Wenceslas

Traditional Carol

Ding, Dong, Merrily on High

English Carol

The Rocking Carol

English Carol

8

Once in Royal David's City

English Carol

Silent Night

Franz Gruber 1818

While Shepherds Watched Their Flocks

Traditional

Away in a Manger

Two Traditional Melodies

Jingle Bells

J. Pierpont

O Come, All Ye Faithful

Adeste Fideles

John Francis Wade, 1743

Deck the Halls

English Carol

The Holly and the Ivy

English Carol

Here We Come A-Wassailing

English Carol

We Wish You a Merry Christmas

Traditional Carol